Rose is a survivor. Her remarkable life began in a tiny Russian village, took her to Warsaw's ghettos and a ship called *The Exodus* and finally to the boardwalks of Atlantic City, the Arizona Canyons and salsa-flavoured nights in Miami Beach.

The play is a portrait of a feisty Jewish woman and a reminder of some of the events that shaped the twentieth century.

Martin Sherman was born in Philadelphia and educated at Boston University. His plays include: *Bent* (Royal Court Theatre, London, 1979; subsequently, West End and Broadway); *Messiah* (Hampstead Theatre, London, 1983); *What She Danced* (Guildford/King's Head Theatre, London, 1988); *A Madhouse in Goa* (Lyric Hammersmith, London, 1989); *Some Sunny Day* (Hampstead Theatre, 1996). Films include: *Clothes in the Wardrobe* (BBC Television, 1992; subsequent cinema release in the US under the title of *The Summer House*, 1994); *Alive and Kicking* (1997); *Bent* (1998). He has lived in London since 1980.

Published by Methuen 1999

3 5 7 9 10 8 6 4

First published in the United Kingdom in 1999 by
Methuen Publishing Limited
215 Vauxhall Bridge Road, London, SW1V 1EJ

Peribo Pty Ltd, 58 Beaumont Road, Mount Kuring-Gai,
NSW 2080, Australia, ACN 002 273 761
(for Australia and New Zealand)

Copyright © 1999 by Martin Sherman

Methuen Publishing Limited Reg. No. 3543167

A CIP catalogue record for this book is available from the British Library

ISBN 0 413 74050 1

Typeset by SX Composing DTP, Rayleigh, Essex
Printed and bound in Great Britain
by Cox & Wyman Ltd, Reading, Berkshire

Papers used by Methuen Publishing Limited are natural, recyclable
products made from wood grown in sustainable forest. The manufacturing
processes conform to environmental regulations of the country of origin.

Caution

Martin Sherman

ROSE

For Elizabeth Shapiro

Methuen

Rose was first performed in the Cottesloe auditorium at the Royal National Theatre on 19 May 1999. The cast was as follows:

Rose   Olympia Dukakis

Directed by Nancy Meckler
Designed by Stephen Brimson Lewis
Lighting by Johanna Town

Rose *sits on a wooden bench. She is eighty. There is a bottle of water and a glass on the bench, as well as a refridgerated pack. Occasional noise can be heard outside.*

Rose   She laughed. And then she blew her nose. She had a cold. The bullet struck her forehead. It caught her in the middle of a thought. She was nine.

Pause.

I'm sitting shivah. You sit shivah for the dead.

Pause.

Shivah sounds like the name of a Hindu god. Maybe it is. I had a flirtation with Oriental religion once. I envied the true Buddhists; they were able to reincarnate; not like us – when we're dead, we're dead; this life, that's it – it's the Jewish curse, we don't have heaven or hell and we don't come back – it's now or never. Of course, for me, now is hardly here any more. I'm eighty years old. I find that unforgivable and suddenly it's a millennium and I stink of the past century, but what can I do? I'm inching towards dust, and sometimes I wish it would hurry, preferably in the middle of a thought, or a sentence, just like that, although not by a bullet to the forehead. And then I wonder if anyone will sit shivah for me; maybe in this bright new twenty-first century they won't sit shivah any more. Well, the ultra-Orthodox will, of course, but something like shivah, in reality, doesn't have much to do with religion, it's just Jewish. You sit on a wooden bench for a week, you laugh, cry, argue as you remember the dead, the particular dead of this particular shivah, and you eat a lot, and kvetch a lot, and you get a sore behind, and it reminds you that you belong to a people, a race, a culture of sore behinds and complainers and heated discussions, of minds in turmoil and minds in flight and minds exploding like the atom, which I still don't understand, but it changed the world, well, it changed the last century, the world that was, and Albert Einstein came from the same street in Germany as my second husband's cousin, what can I tell you? Maybe this past century will be in fact the next to last century, and will it all be because a restless people produce restless minds; when you don't belong anyplace, your mind doesn't belong anyplace, you're owned by no one, except God, and God is only an idea, and so if you believe in God, you have to believe in ideas; except now, who believes in God except the fanatically committed, and if that's true, who believes in ideas? Now is different, anyhow; we don't wander any more; we have a home.

Pause.

I can't catch my breath.

She tries to control her breath. Her problem is very quiet, almost unseen, but she can feel it. She pours a glass of water.

At my age, breathing is one of the few pleasures I have left.

She sips the water.

The elderly are supposed to remember the past with dreadful clarity, but the present – hardly at all. With me, it's not so true. I have only vague, wandering images of my childhood, but yesterday – I remember every single thing about yesterday. Nothing happened yesterday. Trust me. But seventy, seventy-five years ago – Yultishka – a lot happened, but I'm not so sure what. I see Yultishka clearly in my dreams; the subconscious is like an elephant, it never forgets; but when I'm awake, what do I remember? Mud roads. Tiny dwellings, I'm not going to call them houses exactly, but I'm not going to say huts, so – dwellings. Pink trees, well, the blossoms were pink. And carts and wagons. Lots of coming and going; traffic, I suppose, but no exhaust fumes. We had an ozone layer then; it's a shame no one told us, we could have enjoyed it. Yultishka, just a little pimple on the face of the Ukraine, you could squeeze it and it would burst. Just like all the other shtetls, the little Jewish towns that clung by the side of the larger Russian communities; well, sometimes Russian, sometimes Polish; the goyim kept killing each other and – what do they call it? – usurping sovereignty.

Laughs.

Sovereignty! The Ukraine! Why would anyone want it? And today? What would it be like today? Yultishka, if it existed still, wouldn't be that far from Chernobyl. But, in 1920, when I was born, it was Russian. There was a civil war going on, as usual, this time just between Russians, Red and White. By the time I was two, there was famine. But there was always a plate on our table. My mother made sure of that. She took in washing, and with the pennies she made from that she bought fruit from a goyisha farmer and sold the fruit from a little stand on the roadside, and with those pennies, she bought us food. I'll tell you the truth, I've never understood why she couldn't buy the food with the money from the washing. How much less was it than the money from the fruit? But that would have been simple and without strain and she wouldn't have been a martyr. My mother was a saint. Everyone in the shtetl said so. Which is very curious, because sainthood is not a Jewish concept. It's not even a Jewish word. She never complained. She never questioned. God had dropped a genuine Christian into the middle of this shtetl and didn't tell anyone. I was born into a contradiction. My mother's milk was never what it seemed. So the saint – Saint Trebele – was the sole support of her family – my older brother, Asher, my little sister, Rivka, and of course, Rosala, the middle one, that's me.

Who am I forgetting? Papa. Oh papa! Papa was tall and actually quite a beauty, especially his eyes, which were always laughing, although none of us ever got the joke. Shortly after Rivka was born, papa announced he was dying, and took to bed. He was in bed for years and years. He never stopped dying, but as far as we could tell, there was nothing wrong with him. Next to his bed was a large wardrobe, which was filled with medicine bottles, most of them empty, and herbal remedies, most of them used, and none of them able to cure this mysterious illness, which was very much like God, there was no visible sign of it, but some fanatical Jew kept saying it existed. Doctors used to come from neighbouring villages – they were always melancholy –

and they brought medicine as gifts – papa never paid for his hopeless cures – and people from the surrounding area, not all of them Jewish, brought him home-made remedies. He was almost – if you can imagine this in the Ukraine – a tourist attraction. The rabbi came and said blessings once a week, and the effort of listening so exhausted papa he had to sleep through the next day. And the village cabbalists came once a week as well and talked of the devil and mentioned exorcism, which made papa smile, he had a soft spot for hocus-pocus. But the saint, whose religion was more traditional, threw them out – once a week. Mama truly believed in goodness; more than that – if you were Jewish, you had a responsibility to be good; you were, in fact, put on earth to perpetuate a moral force. There was only black and white with her, which, ironically, just made her seem more Christian.

By the time I was ten I was selling fruit on the road. Asher taught me to read Russian as well as Yiddish; I had an ear for languages. Every day I made new signs describing the fruit, which did not need description; you could see them easily enough; melon and berries were luscious then; I can only imagine what they're like today in what was once Yultishka, mutating from fallout. Asher went to the Yeshiva; it was honourable if a boy studied. This annoyed me as I had an overwhelming appetite for knowledge – well, for most things other than science. I read everything I could lay my hands on. I fell in love with words. I memorized large Russian words and invented new Yiddish ones. I became pretentious in several languages at once. Asher came home and discussed the Talmud with me; we had discussions and arguments long into the night, the kind girls were not supposed to have, and I learned then that Judaism's greatest contribution to mankind was asking questions that can't be answered, and that the glory of our race has less to do with giving the world Moses and Marx and Jesus, but everything to do with the invention of the phrase 'on the other hand'. The saint was not impressed by our nocturnal discussions, but then nothing seemed to move her, at least not to appreciation. She never kissed us or touched us or teased us; she never said we were good-looking or sweet-natured; she had no pride in us whatsoever; all of her energy was spent in keeping us alive. She hated answering questions; she had to, of course, when I had my first period; she said it was God's curse, in which she was supported by the Bible. Asher, however, said, on the other hand, it might be God's gift, although he never quite explained why, and I said if that were true I'd rather God had just given me a calendar. So I learned an important lesson that night – God's curses are bad enough, but boy, watch out for His gifts. Shortly after that, the Cossacks came. I suppose if you have your first period and your first pogrom within the same month, you can safely assume childhood is over.

Years later, a history professor told me they couldn't have been Cossacks; Stalin has pacified the Cossacks, he said. Well, there were a few left over. They had big horses and big hats and big whips – everything was big – and beautiful faces; at least that's my memory, but I'm not sure if my memory is of the actual event or a scene from the movie *Fiddler on the Roof*; in my mind, it's exactly like the movie, or maybe the movie was exactly like the event. I close my eyes and I see chorus boys on horses, there's nothing I can do about it, but it's hard to reach my age and to have lived through some of the most tumultuous events of this century and to make clear distinctions between reality and the depictions of reality that constantly surround us. Actually, they were nicer in life than in the movie, because they didn't seem to want to kill anyone, they just wanted to frighten us. It was a bit like the Ku Klux Klan riding into a small southern town wearing sheets, except, of course, I only know that from the movies as well. And so they rode through the villages and broke windows and set fire to stores. They came into our house and we cowered behind a stove, and they didn't try to harm us, they just smashed everything up and rode away. Asher was shouting, Rivka was crying, I was doing a little of both as befits the middle child. Mama, of course, said nothing. She found a broom.

She started cleaning up. It was then that Asher and Rivka and I had the same thought – for in the fuss, there was something we had all forgotten. Papa! We shouted his name. Mama sighed and walked into the bedroom. When she came out she picked up the broom and continued sweeping. Papa's dead, she said. Asher, Rivka and I ran into the bedroom, and we saw that the wardrobe had collapsed on to the bed. Papa's hand was sticking out from under the wardrobe holding an enema bag. We could make out a leg as well, covered with ointments made of rosemary and honey. He had been crushed to death by medicine. Years later, when I became an agnostic, that memory would, just for a second, make me believe in God again.

She sips some water.

Papa's was my first shivah. So many people came we ran out of wooden benches. I think they needed proof that papa had finally died. Mama was in her element, totally impassive. It was God's will.

A few weeks later, on a hot afternoon, I sold the last grapefruit and went for a walk in the woods. I came upon a field covered with lilac trees. I heard a voice. Someone was singing, singing in an unknown tongue – a gypsy melody; no, it was Muslim; no, totally Hebraic; no, wait, I think Spanish, or maybe African – I couldn't tell – or perhaps it was from the moon. It summoned lovers and demons. I crept toward the field. I had to see who was making this delirious sound. Finally, I spotted a fragile figure holding on to a tree; holding, holding and swaying at the same time. I hid behind a bush and listened to the melody and suddenly the figure turned, and I saw its face, covered with sweat and dirt and desire and longing . . . It was mama. I ran. I ran into the woods. I ran away from her song. I ran back to the shtetl. When mama returned home, she was scrubbed and cool, and she wore her saintly face. She started to cook.

Pause.

I never thought of her as Christian again.

I had to escape Yultishka. But Asher beat me to it. He married. From the next village, her name was Chaya, she was a catch, her family were merchants, she had even studied at a school. Her parents gave them money and with it they moved to Warsaw. Asher left me with the fruitstand and the sister and the mother who was really a pagan . . . and each day I grew a little and each day I died a little, both at the same time. I did not belong.

I wrote to Asher. I wrote every week. I begged him to send for me. I begged him to rescue me. I did not belong. I had fevers, I had a cold. My ear hurt. I had spots. My nose ran. I dreamed. I sat in a corner. I watched mama. Mama ignored me.

Asher wrote and said come. Come, if you can. He had a child now. Chaya could use help around the house. Come if you can. He wrote to mama. Send Rosala to Warsaw. She can take a train from Kiev. Send her to Warsaw. Mama looked at me. A dry, cold look. The same look. Always that look. I was desolate. I knew there was no money for a train. Mama went into the bedroom and returned with a scarf. Orange and blue. Like the scarf of a magician; wave it and a rabbit appears. There wasn't a rabbit. There were kopeks instead, hidden inside. I saved, mama said, for when it's life or death. But going to Warsaw, Mama, it's not really life or death. She looked at me. The same look. Always that look. Yes it is, she said.

She holds her chest.

Maybe it's in my mind. Maybe there's nothing wrong with my breathing. Maybe I just panic. Maybe I should drink some water.

She pours another glass of water, and begins to sip it.

The first time I couldn't catch my breath? 1937. Summer. The café on Krochmalna Street. Chaos. Prostitutes and artists and pickpockets and those strange little men who sold lottery tickets – you could, if you were lucky, win an American eagle made of chocolate or three coloured pencils

– and waiters shouting abuse and talk and noise and the possibility, always, of some kind of seduction; and though everyone spoke Polish, and I wasn't yet as fluent as I wanted to be, I felt almost – not quite – comfortable. Asher and his friends from the magazine they worked for were drunk and laughing; Chaya was in a good mood for once; and the room seemed to go around and around, as if we were all in spin-dry. I suppose it was the wine; we were celebrating my first year in Warsaw. And then the spin cycle abruptly stopped and a large man with long red hair was standing at our table. He looked like a gypsy, he had a huge earring in his ear, and his shirt was open, and there was no hair on his chest – no hair! – every man in Warsaw was hairy – and he had one perfect blue eye and one eye of glass, one dead little island in the middle of such life, and Asher was introducing him to me, and I knew, without a doubt, that there would never be anyone else.

We made love that night, surrounded by canvas; paintings, Yussel's paintings, paintings of shtetls, of tiny villages with mud roads and lilac trees; imitation Yultishkas surrounded me in that garret in Warsaw where I was finally free and finally a woman. Once when I was a child I heard the bedsprings in the bedroom rocking and thumping but there was no other sound, no human voice; it must have been the night Rivka was conceived, and I lay in the front room terrified, terrified by that silence. But with Yussel and me there was such noise – moaning and screaming and laughing and gasping – oh no – no . . .

She waves her hand away.

I don't want to remember.

Pause.

And we lived happily ever after.

She takes a long drink of water.

Yussel wasn't a bad artist. He wasn't exactly a Chagall, but then, who is? Jews aren't visual – look at what they wear. I suppose it's because we were never allowed to reproduce an image of God, unlike the goyim, who love the naked bodies of men caught in some kind of sado-masochistic ecstasy, strung up on a piece of wood or with an arrow piercing a nipple. But sex and God are very confused for goyim; for Jews they're separate. We can't see our God, so we can't desire Him. And when He abandons us, as He always does, we feel betrayed by a parent, not by a lover. Or maybe, like a parent. One day He just dies. So, believe me, when I was in bed with Yussel, there was no religious dimension. Actually, he was insatiable. He had to have everything today, as if tomorrow didn't even exist as a concept. Maybe he knew.

When we weren't making love, we were at the movies, especially if they showed a western. We loved cowboys and injuns and canyons and the Rio Grande and stagecoaches riding round the bend and tumbleweed rolling into an empty town – could that have been real? We liked musicals too, particularly the silly Yiddish ones, with Molly Picon dancing around a shtetl, singing –

Sings.

'Yiddle mit a fiddle . . .
Yiddle, Yiddle, Yiddle . . .'

We walked the streets of Warsaw with our friends, arguing and dreaming and laughing and the goyim passing by would look at us with discomfort and even resentment, and one night, walking across the Kravidjin Bridge, I heard about Palestine for the first time, the land of our ancestors, the land that God promised us, and I giggled, because, even then, I knew about God's promises. Yussel would lean over and gently bite my ear and then nothing else mattered.

Sometimes Yussel would sell a painting, but he didn't make much of a living; the last thing he needed was a wife, but now, suddenly, he had a wife, and a year later, a child. I named her Esther, she had red hair like her father, and *two* blue eyes.

I don't know how Yussel lost his eye, he refused to tell me, but occasionally, in the middle of the night, he would start to scream and I would hold him and stroke his brow, and then Esther would start to cry and I'd have to go to her, and in the morning he'd accuse me of deserting him and of not caring about his pain, and I would say but I don't know what your pain is, and he would say I was blind, and I would bite my tongue and not say well, actually, in reality, you're blind, half-blind, and I don't know why. When we made love he would plunge into me, but I could never enter him, not really; emotionally, I was allowed foreplay, nothing else, and I felt, here, in the closest relationship I would ever have, still outside, like that tumbleweed rolling through an empty town, and suddenly I would miss Yultishka and worry about mama and Rivka and then lie awake at night listening to the soldiers marching outside.

When the Nazis first entered Warsaw it didn't mean anything to me. It was someone else's war. I liked Warsaw, but I had no affection for Poland. How much worse could the Germans be? Well, I can't help it, I really did think that, what did I know?

I don't remember the ghetto.

Pause.

Well – OK – packed together. They took us from our homes. They relocated us into one small area and built a wall around us. There were twelve Jews to a room. Twelve – twelve – to a room. But I don't remember it. Maybe it wasn't twelve. I don't know. I'll tell you what hell is – it's twelve people snoring at the same time. Maybe I'm imagining it. Yussel had his bad dreams all the time now. I didn't have bad dreams. You have to sleep to have dreams. I was afraid to sleep. I was afraid something would happen to Esther if I slept. How had this happened? We had only yesterday been walking across the Kravidjin Bridge. We had been in a café just a month ago eating chocolate cake. Cake. Now there was a half chicken for the entire room. Twelve people. Maybe it wasn't twelve. What was going on? Who was this man with red hair and an earring? What was I doing with him? I should have been selling grapefruit on a road. And then there wasn't a half chicken any more. We were starving.

I searched for my brother. I found him at the other end of the ghetto. Asher and Chaya were living with nine other people. Their child had died. The cholera. Chaya was screaming when I entered the room. Asher told me to ignore her but I couldn't. I tried to comfort her. She called me a bitch. She pulled my hair. I slapped her. Soon I was screaming. I don't know why. They had no food. Asher said he had contacts who could find me a job in a factory outside the ghetto. The owner was friendly to Jews and took in more than she needed, but only women. Chaya started to beat her breasts. Asher grabbed a rope and tied her hands. I saw how thin he was. Why were we in Warsaw? Chaya started to vomit. The other people in the room cursed her. I ran out into the night air. There was no air. Back in my room, Yussel stared at the ceiling. Esther was telling herself a story. She was three. We had a few bread crusts for all of us, for twelve people. Maybe it wasn't twelve. I took Yussel's hand. Where were you, why did you desert me, he said.

I started work at the factory. They let you out of the ghetto in the morning and escorted you back at night. Yussel didn't want me to leave, but we needed the food. It was possible for women to smuggle scraps of food back into the ghetto; the young soldiers at the gate were strangely shy about body searches. One afternoon, in the factory, we heard noise coming from the ghetto. We ran to the window. We could see the ghetto wall. Smoke was rising behind the wall. We heard screaming in the distance. Screaming. No, we didn't. I don't remember what we heard. Some of the factory women fainted. My body lost control. I shat myself. Esther and Yussel were in the ghetto. I ran to the bathroom. Cold water didn't help. I wanted to go to sleep. The screaming grew louder. No, it didn't. I don't remember. We had to go back to our machines.

That night we returned to the ghetto. The streets were filled
with bodies. Buildings were burning. SS men were walking
with dogs. I found my room; everything in it had been
smashed to pieces. It was empty. Where were Esther and
Yussel? I walked the streets calling Esther's name, passing
other mothers calling the names of their children; a giant
chorale of names filled the ghetto under the red sky. Years
later someone offered me LSD; I said I didn't have to take
it, I knew what it was like, hallucinating; a minute stretched
out into an hour, strange visions soaring through your mind
and then disappearing, the feeling you will never come back
down to reality. I knew what it was like. I found a space
where Asher's room had been. It was gone. Asher was gone.
Chaya was gone. A hand pulled me off of the sidewalk. It
was Simka, a man from our room. He had hidden in a cellar
in another part of the ghetto. When the raid began, he was
in our room. Yussel had handed Esther to him and said take
her to the cellar. But Yussel had stayed behind. How could
he slip through the streets unnoticed with his red hair and
his earring?

Why did he wear an earring? Did he think he was a gypsy? I
wanted to tear it from his ear until the ear bled. He said to
Simka, tell her, tell my wife, my Rosala, to protect our
daughter. That was it. Thank you very much, Yussel, love of
my life. Later someone told me they saw him marching in
the left line of prisoners, the line of useless people, the line
for one-eyed men, the line that led to the clearing in the
wood, where the machine-guns were. Fertilizer. They
turned the bodies into fertilizer. What did they do with the
earring? I don't remember any of this.

Simka and Esther started running through the streets.
Simka did not look at me when he talked. He closed his
eyes. He said they passed a soup kitchen. The Jewish
Committee were handing out soup. Esther broke away from
Simka. Simka covered his face when he talked. Esther ran
toward the soup. They had never distributed soup before. A
Ukranian soldier was passing by. A young blond Ukranian.
Maybe he was a neighbour from Yultishka. Stalin and

Hitler were friends now, for a minute; the Ukraines helped
the Germans guard the ghetto. But why soup today? The
soldier had a small gun. Simka said it again and again, a
small gun, as if the size was important. Esther ran for the
soup. The soldier aimed his gun, the small gun. Esther
reached the soup. The soldier pulled the trigger. I suppose
the trigger was small too. The bullet hit her forehead. He
might have been from Yultishka. He was just passing by.
Simka started to cry. Esther lay dead in front of the soup.
Mostly water, it wasn't really soup. I kicked Simka in the
stomach. I was supposed to protect her. Thank you very
much, Yussel. Simka fell to the ground. I ran back into the
street. I don't know what happened next.

Pause.

If I were Buddhist this would give me points. On account
for the next life.

Pause.

It's almost time for my pill. For the breathing.

Pause.

I sat shivah in the sewers. There were no wooden benches,
but God makes allowances. Except I stopped believing in
God. God died in the ghetto; when I kicked Simka; just
about then. On the other hand, I still needed ritual. So I sat
a kind of mental shivah. For Esther. For Yussel. For Asher.
For mama. For Rivka. I knew in my heart that mama and
Rivka were gone as well. Later I met someone from a village
near Yultishka who described the end of our shtetl. The
Nazis marched all the Jews into the schoolhouse, locked the
doors, and burnt it down. Easy. Screams behind the walls.
Again. I sat that kind of shivah for two years. I don't really
know how I got to the sewers, that's a blank. But once there,
oh, I remember everything. There were about thirty of us. I
was numb. Novocaine. Two years. You do things to stay
alive . . . I remember . . . everything . . .

She takes the glass of water and drinks it very slowly.

She does not speak.

A long pause.

This I will say. We talked of Jerusalem. We were by the
waters of Babylon, beneath Warsaw, and we remembered
Zion. The promised land. Promised. Our own. No one
elses. No Cossacks. No Nazis. Just us. Safe.

Well, then. The war was over. One day Nazis were
marching into Warsaw. Another day, Russians. One day
Stalin and Hitler were buddies. Another day, enemies. It
had nothing to do with us. My mind couldn't absorb facts.
Facts no longer made sense. My head was filled with images,
with jump-cuts. Nothing was linear. I tried not to have
memories. I was still numb, but my feet worked. I got out of
there. Away from the Russians. I had to go someplace safe.
Where was safe? Oh yes. Germany was safe. Long lines of
refugees, passing through Poland, rushing toward the
country that destroyed them. That was now itself destroyed.
We passed through Dresden. A child with no arms crawled
through the streets. The streets were rubble. The goodies
had conquered the baddies, and had saved what remained
of our lives, but the child had no arms. I found the
Americans. They welcomed us. They gave us cigarettes. I
had never smoked before. I smoked for the next fifty years.
Now I can't catch my breath. They gave us soup. They put
us in a camp. They called it a centre but, believe me, it was
a camp. A nice camp, not a bad camp, but still, a camp.
Barbed wire and bunk beds. The war was over. What was I
doing in a camp? In Germany, where it's safe? I was
officially called a displaced person. I could have told them
that a long time before.

The camps were overcrowded. No one knew what to do
with us. We had no homes to return to. But I had a place to
go. I had Palestine. I was adopted by the Zionists in the
camp. I was a heroine. Hadn't I fought back in the ghetto?
Actually, no. I hadn't; when the ghetto rose up in its last
gasp of fury, I was already in the sewers. But I let them

believe what they wanted to believe. They were my ticket
out.

One day the smugglers arrived. High-priced criminals, paid
for by the Haganah. They bribed the soldiers. Two hundred
people were selected from our camp. Some wore three pairs
of clothing on top of one another and carried a knapsack. I
travelled light. I had nothing. Soap and a towel. We climbed
through a hole in the fence. The soldiers closed their eyes.
The smugglers never smiled. We climbed into trucks. The
trucks sped into the night. Some people screamed. They
remembered the Nazi trucks. They thought it was a trick.
But the next night we were in France. In Sete, by the sea. I
had never seen the sea. It was just another image, another
hallucination. A boat was in harbour. It was falling apart.
We were marched aboard, like cattle, herds of us, mooing
and rushing and falling in the dark. We were being rustled,
like in *Red River* and only caution kept the smugglers from
shouting Yippee-I-O. But once on board we were no longer
cattle. We were now sardines. If you turned around, your
elbow hit a nose. The boat set sail and secretly negotiated its
way out of the harbour. The French turned a blind eye. The
British were determined to stop us from going to Palestine.
The British had won Palestine on the Monopoly board, you
see, and they were trying to hold on both to it and their
dignity. Their foreign minister was named Bevin and he was
the goy from hell. He only allowed fifteen hundred Jews a
month into the Holy Land; certain basic facts about the war
seemed to have passed him by. The Haganah were trying to
sneak as many Jews as possible into the country, although
sneak is hardly the word; we were a creaky old boat on the
open seas, difficult to miss, and within a day we were being
tailed by British warships.

The mood on board the boat had changed. We were
allowed on to the open deck and suddenly there was an
accordian and the sardines were singing and dancing. I
heard melody. The Mediterranean was playful, the waves
hypnotic, and for a moment, the numbness began to wear
away. Then I saw children throwing a ball, a little girl

playing hide-and-seek, a tiny girl, and I couldn't bear it. I closed my eyes. I didn't want to remember. I didn't want the quick sharp images in my brain and I was angry at Yussel, at Yussel, for wearing an earring.

I opened my eyes. I saw a man's chest, a hairless chest. What was the point of opening my eyes if the images remained? Then I realized the chest was attached to a sailor who was smiling at me. Why was he smiling at me? There was a chill from the sea. He put on his shirt, but he was clumsy, and he put his head into the hole for his arm, and he was stuck. The ship was run by sailors who couldn't navigate a shirt. Suddenly my body was seized by convulsions. My spine went into spasm, my stomach jumped. I felt an electric current run through my bosom, and I knew this was it, finally, I was going to die, and I heard a sound from my throat, a strange, heaving sound, and then I realized what was happening. I was laughing. I had forgotten. I hadn't laughed since the café on Krochmalna Street. Something Yussel had said. He kissed my cheek which was wet from tears of laughter. Had that really happened? And now, in another life, on the open sea, this silly sailor with his head in the armhole had made my body scream ha-ha-ha. Who invented that sound, those syllables? If ha-ha-ha is a word, it's the only one that exists in every language. And then the sailor – he who produced ha-ha-ha – winked at me and disappeared into the crowd.

He returned that evening. We were still on the open deck. He sat beside me, or rather, fell beside me; he tripped on a rope holding a pail of water and splashed the water over us. We were squeezed together, refugees on either side. He was flirting with me, at least I think he was; I had no experience of flirting; Yussel was very direct – that first night at the café he said I think we should fuck and I blushed but I thought so too and what was the point of pretending otherwise? The sailor's name was Sonny. Sonny Rose. He spoke Yiddish, his parents were from a village not far from mine, but he was born in America. Most of the sailors were American volunteers. None of them had experience on a boat, but they too had dreams of Palestine. They didn't have to be on the ship; we did; and that made me like him. I asked if he was from the West, with Indians and tumbleweed, but he said no, New Jersey. I liked him a little less. When I told him my name he said oh what a shame, we can never marry, you would be Rose Rose. I'm not sure that my face showed it, but in some way, I think I smiled.

Mr Bevin didn't smile, though. His warships moved closer. Someone said they were destroyers. The next morning the sailors hung a flag across the top of the boat. It had the Star of David on it. And a sign as well, a sign that renamed the ship. It said: *Exodus 1947*. I can see that sign so clearly. But, of course, how could I then, standing underneath it? Am I remembering the newsreels or the movie with Paul Newman? Or did I crank my neck? How can I tell? Sonny helped put the sign up, but he lost his footing, and dangled from the Star of David until his laughing shipmates helped him down.

We were nearing land, promised land. Only nearing, we were still in international waters, which were supposedly safe. That night the warships moved to our side. They squeezed us. Then they rammed us. We heard English voices on megaphones. What were they saying? Then there was tear gas. British sailors wearing steel helmets boarded the boat. They had clubs. We had soda pop. The Haganah had loaded our hardest food supplies on deck for us to fight with. Refugees were hurling cans of kosher corned beef at the steel helmets. I saw one of the sailors being clubbed. I saw a boy, only sixteen, his family wiped out in the camps, shot in the face. He died with Palestine on his lips. I picked up a potato. I threw the potato. Suddenly everything that had happened in the past seven years released itself through potatoes. I was no longer numb. I threw potatoes for my child, I threw potatoes for Yussel, for mama. I was screaming. I was exhilarated. I was almost happy. And my aim was good. I was wiping out Mr Bevin's Boys. I saw someone aim a gun at me, and then suddenly I was on the ground. Sonny had thrown me down. A bullet whizzed

above us. Sonny dragged me into a corner, away from the
fighting. He kissed me. His lips tasted of flesh. Yussel's
tasted of cherry vodka. I've just saved your life, he said. I
looked at him. I hated him for it.

The British had the boat, rather the hulk, the remains of the
boat. The Royal Navy towed us into the harbour. We were
entering Palestine at last, but we were under arrest. We
started to sing 'Hatikvah'. Listen, 'Hatikvah' is not exactly
the 'Marseillaise'; like most national anthems it goes on too
long and no one knows the words. So we made up words.
Then we heard the real words coming from the shore.
Jewish settlers were waiting for us on the dock and they
were singing. Our voices blended together. It was yet
another hallucination, another LSD trip, except this one
had a musical score. Sonny grabbed my hand. He was
crying. All the Americans were crying. But the refugees
didn't cry. We were too tired. Was it ever going to end?

We landed. The mandate police came on board and took us
off the boat in single lines. Goodbye, sardines, back to cattle.
Palestine didn't seem like much. It was dirty and hot and
there were insects everywhere and strange-looking Arabs in
robes and headgear and camels and jeeps and the settlers
cheering us as we marched by and suddenly the woman in
front of me fell to the ground and kissed the earth and
screamed Palestine, and I thought what a sentimental fool
she was, and then I felt dirt grazing my chin and I realized I
was on the ground too and my lips were touching the dirt
and I thought the earth tasted of cherry vodka but that was
in my mind and I didn't know why I was on the ground or
why I had started to cry and I felt a policeman pull me up
and march me back into the line.

We were hungry, but they didn't feed us. We were thirsty,
but they didn't offer us water. Instead they sprayed us for
lice. For years after I thought if the British invite you to their
house they spray you first. And then they marched us to
another ship and we sailed away from Palestine. It had been
a mirage, five hours in the Promised Land, a stopover on

the cruise ship, a quick package tour to salvation. Now we were headed for Cyprus, where they had – guess what? – camps, camps for illegal immigrants. The Americans were on our boat as well and the next morning Sonny, who understood a compass, realized we were not sailing to Cyprus after all. We were on the open seas, heading back to Europe.

Sonny was agitated. *The Exodus* had created a scandal. The entire world was watching us, he said. There were even reporters on board. He didn't stop talking. Why was he talking to me? Why didn't he talk to someone else? He was boring me. I didn't care about a propaganda victory. I just wanted to sleep. In a bed, near mama. I wanted mama. Why didn't he stop talking? He kept taking my hand. I let him. It didn't matter.

We landed in a French port. The French said they would only allow volunteers to disembark. No one volunteered. The Haganah smuggled messages on to the ship saying Do Not Leave. Why would we leave? Where did we have to go? We were taking a stand. I wanted a bed. I didn't care. It was so hot. We were sailing again. We were sardines again. The constant changing from fish to cow and back again had broken my spirit, which had only half existed anyhow, and then only because of Palestine. It was so hot. The reporters filed their dispatches – a homeless people wander from port to port. Mr Bevin had a shit fit. He sent our boat back to Germany. Sonny kept talking. He said the British had overplayed their hand, they had a public relations disaster. I looked at him, stupified; if you have just been through a war in Europe, not to mention a Holocaust, you weren't exactly sure what public relations meant.

We landed again, this time in Hamburg. We refused to disembark. British soldiers burst on to the ship and clubbed us; they were getting quite good at that, and dragged us off of the boat. They took us to a train. A woman screamed when she saw the train had barred windows. I was hustled on to the train. It was chaos. I didn't see Sonny, but he was

American, so he was free. Suddenly there was a lot of steam; the train started to move, very slowly. I saw Sonny on the platform running alongside the train shouting my name. I went to the door which was still open. This is ridiculous, he shouted. Jump off the train. Jump off and marry me. I'll take you to America. And then later we can go to Palestine. Jump. Rose! Jump!

I didn't know what to do. My heart was barely alive; if my body jumped, it wouldn't bring love with it. And maybe I still had a husband. After all, how did I really know that Yussel was dead? Someone saw him marching to the machine-guns, sure, but did they see a body? On the other hand, how could he have survived? But shouldn't I search for him? Just in case? In case of what – a miracle?

Jump, he screamed. The train was leaving the platform. The train to nowhere. At least I think it was leaving. Or was this too a movie? How many times had I watched this scene with the steam and the platform and the lover? Maybe we were still on the boat. America, he cried. I leaned out of the train. I couldn't believe I had a future. America, America! My mind closed down. I shut my eyes. What did it matter? I jumped. He caught me and then dropped me and we rolled over on the platform and then we were surrounded by soldiers with guns and they were shouting at us and I watched the train disappear into the mist, into Europe, into what years later my kind would call The Old Country.

She takes a bag from beneath the wooden bench. She removes a group of medicine bottles from the bag, and lays them, one by one, on the bench.

Papa would be proud. I take medicine now. For the breathing. For the cholesterol. For the kidney. For this and that. I'm doing what papa dreamed of for so long. I'm dying. Not specifically, but when you're eighty you are, in essence, on the way out. Isn't it strange that I'm still alive? How many times I closed my eyes and said now, now, take me now, please. I can't go on. If there is a God, you'll take me now, and in a moment like that I believed in Him, and then when I opened my eyes, I didn't. But God is like a policeman, He's never there when you want him, and then, of course, He arrests you when you're innocent. Why do I spend so much time talking about something I don't believe in?

The problem is I can't swallow pills. Once I choked on an aspirin and almost died and that's not how I want to go, I want to go quietly in the middle of a sentence. So I've been frightened of pills ever since. I envy people who just throw their head back and drop a whole bunch of capsules down their throat. And then swallow and smile. Bastards. So I chew my pills. The problem is they taste like donkey droppings. So I have to kill the taste.

She takes a container of ice cream out of her portable feezer and puts it on her lap. She opens it. She chews a pill, and then eats a few spoonfuls of ice cream, and repeats the process as she talks, until she has finished her medicine.

Peanut butter vanilla. It's a new flavour. I like to be au courant. I know, I know, I'm eating ice cream to take a pill for cholesterol. I'll tell you something – who cares?

The first time I ate ice cream was in Atlantic City. Ice cream and frozen custard. There was a frozen-custard stand on the boardwalk, in front of the burlesque house, near the pier, across from the beach, where I sold chairs. Sonny was born and raised in Atlantic City. I'm sure he told me that on the boat, but I usually wasn't listening to him, and as a result, I knew nothing about him. Or maybe he told me during the endless days when we argued with the soldiers and the immigration officials and the bureaucrats; the days of filling out forms, when all I could think of was why am I here, shouldn't I have stayed on the train, who is this man? The Americans were nice to us, though; Sonny had an uncle in some bureau and finally I received a paper that said I existed, and a Jewish chaplain married us in Berlin, and then I was back on a boat, with a husband who was seasick all the time, which he wasn't on *The Exodus*, and I nursed him and asked myself who – who is he?

Sonny's parents had a few 'who' questions of their own.
Their boy runs away to be a pirate and returns with a
catatonic shtetl girl, when what they always wanted was a
nice Jewish-American daughter-in-law named Sheila or
Arlene, who at the very least spoke English, which is a little
weird if you ask me, as they had never bothered to learn the
language themselves, whereas I became fluent within a year.
But if his parents still spoke Yiddish they were hardly alone;
Atlantic City was Warsaw-on-the-Sea, which was ironic
because if ever a people were not built for bathing suits it
was ours. The air smelled of aspirin and chicken fat and
suntan oil, but the Jews who made the city their summer
playground were the fortunate ones; they had had the good
sense to leave Europe when the going was good. But guilt
hung in the sea air as well, and my presence disturbed them.
They were relieved to discover I did not have a number on
my arm, but they certainly weren't interested in the images
in my brain. They didn't want to know. Not that I wanted
to tell them. Once I overheard a woman say, These people
go on too much about the past; life isn't easy for anyone.
She was wearing a mink coat and it was July. She was a
guest at one of the many palaces that pretended they were
hotels, palaces from another age, a jazz age, a Scott
Fitzgerald age, beautiful and hideous at the same time. The
same minked woman was heard saying, Art deco, art
shmeco, the bathrooms are clean. For one dollar a boy
pushed you on a rolling chair on the boardwalk – a rolling
chair was a chair that rolled, all the terms in Atlantic City
were literal – and you passed the shmeco palaces and the
dancing waters – coloured water that sprouted in different
formations and thus danced – and the Steel Pier, which had
two movie theatres, a vaudeville house, a dance hall and a
diving horse, which was, needless to say, a horse that dived
into the ocean. You passed the Ice Capades, an ice show
that spent each summer in Atlantic City and was thought
exotic because ice-skating was one of those useless things
that only goyim did. You passed the arcades and the
fortune-tellers and the stores selling salt-water taffy, which
ruined Jewish teeth for the next two generations. Sonny took

me on a rolling chair on my first night, and halfway down
the boardwalk we passed a store selling nuts and suddenly
we were approached by a six-foot peanut with a huge
peanut head who danced over to our rolling chair and
kissed me on the forehead and called me little lady and I
knew then that I was foolish to think my hallucinations
would end when I arrived in America and I wondered if I
had survived the sewers of Warsaw so I could be groped by
a giant peanut. Why hadn't I stayed on the train and
returned to a nice sensible displaced person camp?

Sonny's father owned several beach chair concessions and
he gave one to Sonny as a start up the ladder – that was an
American expression – although I couldn't imagine what
beach chairs would lead to. We rented our beach chairs by
the hour to the sunburned crowds; Sonny and I would
schlep the chairs to a designated spot in the blazing heat,
which often meant Sonny tripped over a chair, both of them
flying in several directions at once. He never wore a shirt on
the beach, which was a saving grace, although his body
lacked Yussel's sharp lines. Yussel's this, Yussel's that,
Yussel's report card had straight As, whilst Sonny's was
barely average. At night there were attempts at lovemaking
although he was as clumsy in bed as he was on solid ground,
and I tried not to think of Yussel's penis and I wished the
stranger on top of me wasn't called Sonny because I
couldn't even help him out by faking love-talk when he had
the name of a child. Our lovemaking was silent, like my
parents', and in the morning I was sullen and distant and
cruel. When I became pregnant, I panicked. How could I
have another child, a child I wouldn't be able to protect? I
thought of throwing myself down the stairs, but I could
never act on my baser instincts, and so Abner was born.
Sonny wanted me to name him Asher, but how could I say
Asher every day and remember? Abner was close enough,
and it was so American, it could even be the name of a
cowboy.

Sonny and I still dreamed of Palestine, except it was no
longer Palestine, but Israel, a nation at last, thanks to some

degree to *The Exodus*. The adventures of our pathetic boat
had swung world opinion in favour of creating a new state.
We knew we belonged there, but I couldn't face another
long journey, not just yet. For once in my life I wanted to
stay put, if only for a few years.

Sometimes we would go out at night. There was the Harlem
Follies at the Jockey Club, and the burlesque house, which
was fun, mainly because the comedians were Jewish and
told Jewish jokes. But then the comedians on television were
Jewish as well, and Yiddish words entered the English
language, words like schmuck and schlep and schmatte and
schmooze and chutzpah. We saw Yiddish magicians at the
hotels who pulled little Jewish rabbits out of their hats and
we heard chazanas, female cantors who sang melancholy
shtetl melodies and I would remember the lilac tree and
finally understand. Molly Picon came once to entertain; she
was tiny and depressingly energetic and she sang 'Yiddle mit
a Fiddle' as if she were still simulating shtetl life on a
Warsaw screen.

We went to the Yiddish theatre and saw plays in which
demons and goblins haunted the shtetls, and I remembered
how superstitious we were in Yultishka, how mama would
spit three times if anyone mentioned the dead and how
Satan was as accepted a presence as God. One night we saw
The Dybbuk, a play about a young girl whose body is
possessed by the soul of her dead lover. I was trembling as
the curtain came down. What's wrong, Sonny asked. I
didn't answer. I couldn't bear to look at him. I ran out on to
the boardwalk and then on to the beach and stared at the
ocean which was bathed in moonlight. I could run into the
sea and find that spot where the horizon ended. Sonny
rushed to me and took me in his arms. No, there's another
answer, I thought. I would bring Yussel back to me. I would
make Yussel's spirit possess my body.

If Yussel was really going to possess me, I needed to give
him a push. I decided to dye my hair red and wear one long
gypsy earring as well as trousers, which was not an accepted

fashion for women in those days. Some kind of prudence prevented me from gouging out one eye, I expected Sonny's parents would be outraged by my new appearance, but instead they approved. They thought I looked less Russian, which was a good thing, as, thanks to Senator McCarthy, Russian was definitely out of fashion, and my old more severe look was suspicious. The hysteria over reds under beds was in high gear and actually communist was just a code word for Jew. One congressman even made a speech in the House Of Representatives claiming that communists had betrayed and then killed Jesus, which was, as metaphors go, not too subtle. As Americans were no longer very good on horses, they conducted their pogroms around committee tables and under television lights. I wasn't too concerned about myself; I knew that the politicians were mesmerized by the state department and show business; I didn't think they were panicked about the beach chair industry. Still, Sonny's parents were relieved when I assumed my non-Russian madwoman look. This annoyed me because one of the points about possession is that everyone around you recognizes it. Yussel's persona within me was still only skin-deep.

He needed inducement. I found a book about Cabala and in it the perfect magic spell for summoning a dead spirit. It involved semen, which was tricky, but finally one night, as Sonny fumbled inside of me, I asked him to pull out and come on my stomach. As soon as he had finished I jumped out of bed and scooped up his semen on a piece of cardboard. I ran to the kitchen where I mixed the semen with a chopped chicken neck and olive oil and cloves. Sonny stood in the doorway, watching. I knew he would never forgive me. Instead, he smiled in a way I hadn't seen before. My fascination with his semen was seemingly a boon to his manhood, and my dalliance with a magic potion was so – well – not American, so primitive, so European, so exotic, and after all, isn't that why he had married me and not Stephanie Perlow from Asbury Park? I smeared the potion on the bedroom door. Sonny then offered to assist me, little dreaming he was helping me summon my first husband. But Yussel was curiously uninterested in Sonny's semen; I yearned to have him inside my body, but he just wasn't there yet.

Maybe if I behaved like Yussel it would give him a push in my direction. I started to swagger around the house and I took up painting and once, when Sonny returned from Abner's room where he had been reading him a story, I accused him of deserting me. Sonny's joy was uncontained; he thought I had missed him. OK, I thought, maybe it would help if I noticed women. I remembered walking with Yussel on Grabowska Street which was near the Muranow Theatre and always filled with young actresses. Yussel insisted I walk on his left, so if I looked at him sideways I would only see his glass eye; supposedly I would be unaware that his good eye was checking out every pretty girl that passed. Yussel was never faithful. I didn't admit that then, but now that I was almost him, I knew it was so. Who had he slept with? Were they friends of mine? If only Yussel would come into my body and name names, as if he were in front of Senator McCarthy. One night I placed my hand on Sonny's sister-in-law's right breast. I knew at that moment I had gone too far and the entire family would know that Yussel was trying to return. But his sister-in-law was thrilled; she asked me to meet her the next day on the boardwalk by the cotton-candy stand. The more I became like Yussel, the more everybody liked me. Yussel had become the most popular woman in Atlantic City. But still he eluded me. He wasn't inside.

So then Miss America arrived. The Miss America Pageant officially ended the summer season in Atlantic City and it was a big deal for the beach chair trade since the pageant began with a parade. The beauty queen of every state rolled down the boardwalk on an individual float and, thank God, onlookers had to sit on something. You booked one of our chairs a month in advance, it was that popular. All the ladies from the hotels put on their best summer dresses and oohed and ahhed over the pretty shiksas. The parade began with a little band and then the first girl, Miss Alabama; it was alphabetical. People cheered and whistled and were especially excited if the girl was from their home state; and the perky little Protestant faces glided slowly by.

Abner was playing in and around the chairs; he was three, the dangerous age, the age of Esther, but I felt he was safe as both Yussel and I were looking after him. Yussel wasn't inside of me yet, but he was close. I was convinced he was somewhere in the vicinity. It was a blazing hot day. Sonny decided to buy us cream sodas. He crossed over the boardwalk, in front of Miss Colorado, and disappeared into the crowd. I lay back and closed my eyes. I opened them, saw Miss Delaware, closed them again. Yussel was so close. I knew it. I'm sure he was enjoying the parade. So many pretty girls. Bastard. I began to drift. I awoke to hear Abner screaming daddy, daddy. I looked across the boardwalk, as Miss Iowa waved to me. Sonny was lurching through the crowd on the other side. He was holding three cans of cream soda. He dropped one can. He picked it up. He dropped another. He lost his balance. He stepped on a woman's foot. She screamed. He dropped the third can. People were laughing at him. He started to cross to us, but he lurched again and collided with Miss Massachusetts, or rather, the bottom of her float. He was down for the count. Miss Massachusetts didn't miss a beat, she just kept waving and smiling and ignoring the funny man sprawled on the ground. Someone in the crowd shouted the guy's drunk. But I knew that wasn't true; Sonny never touched alcohol. And, then, in a flash, it happened. What I had been waiting for. The Miracle. I felt a shudder near my heart. Someone was pushing his way into my body. It was Yussel. Yussel had come at last. Yussel had taken possession. Miss New Hampshire looked at me as she went past; had she seen Yussel dive inside of me? In the distance I saw Miss New York and I wondered if she would shout dybbuk, dybbuk. The crowd applauded. But it wasn't as I imagined. I thought I would hear Yussel's voice, perhaps even speak with his voice, and certainly, I would think his thoughts. But

no, he took possession with his eye. He entered my own eyes
and they saw through his one good one. My eyes – Yussel's
eye – brought Sonny into sharp focus and saw that Sonny
wasn't clumsy, after all, and Sonny certainly wasn't drunk.
Yussel's eye saw that Sonny was ill, that Sonny had some
kind of disease, that Sonny was now maybe dying. I took a
deep breath. I ran to Sonny and helped him up. Don't know
what's wrong, sweetheart, he said. It's nothing, it's just the
sun, I said, but inside of me, inside, I said Yussel – goodbye,
because I knew that now he had to leave and leave for ever,
and I felt his good eye release its hold on my brain and I felt
his spirit lift up through my body and out of my body and
fly over Miss Oregon and Miss Pennsylvania and fly further
still until it was over the Steel Pier and its diving horse and
fly even further until it had disappeared into the humid New
Jersey air.

Pours another glass of water.

What's the point of taking a pill if it doesn't help? I think my
pills are made of sugar. My doctor says there's no problem
with my breathing. If there was, he says, I wouldn't talk so
much. You'll drop dead talking, he says. He's trying to
frighten me. Believe me, it's an inducement.

Sips the water.

OK. So. Eight years later I owned a hotel in Miami Beach.
Well, that's America, isn't it? Go figure. What could I do? I
had a husband who required a lot of medical care.
Americans tend to think of illness as unhealthy. It costs. So I
had to go out and hustle.

I took a job ordering food for the Majestic Hotel. Soon I
was running the kitchen. Soon I was managing the place.
The guests loved me. I understood them and their
complaints and I was pleasant when I had to be and cruel
when it was necessary and it was easy because it allowed me
to protect Sonny, and Abner as well, and I could do for
them what I failed to do for Esther. Maybe that's why
Yussel's eye had showed me the truth. Maybe. Who knows.

Sonny's was a rare neurological disorder; it had been building slowly through the years – when he fell at my feet on the ship he was not only manifesting love – and now it would accelerate. Motion, speech and thought would slowly disintegrate. The doctors could do nothing. Sonny was as devastated by the knowledge of the disease as the disease itself. Cigarettes became his passion, his profession, his art form. He sat at the kitchen table. He would drop a cigarette on the table, pick it up, drop it again, pick it up – the table became a mosaic of burns and the burns represented some kind of pleasure. Sometimes I gave him sexual relief. I wanted to surround him with an illusion of love.

Our dreams, our fantasies, about Israel had started to grow again before my obsession with the dybbuk, but now they had to be tucked away, like Sonny's personality, into a distant closet.

Abner grew; we called him Abbie now; and by the time he was seven his thin little voice would make the evening announcement over the Majestic loudspeaker – The dining room is now open for dinner – as the dining-room doors flung open to a stampede; it was every man for himself as the hotel guests desperately rushed toward that evening's special brisket or smoked whatever.

The guests were intrigued by me because of *The Exodus*. That gave me cachet; it spelled adventure, unlike the death camps, which were still too dark and threatening to be thought about. A boat they could deal with. I didn't tell them about anything else. Nor did I tell Abbie about the ghetto, or even Yultishka. I made sure that the guests never spoke directly to him in Yiddish. I wanted Abbie to be an all-American boy. I obsessively devoured books during the night, but kept that a secret vice. I no longer dressed like a demented gypsy. My suddenly tasteful wardrobe stood out from the clashing colours favoured by the Majestic clientele. They knew I didn't quite belong. But what finally cemented my popularity was the one true gift that Sonny had given me, if you don't count my life, and that was my name. Who could forget Rose Rose?

What people did forget was Majestic. Soon they were saying we're going to Rose Rose's for the summer. That is, those who still came to Atlantic City. There were now black ghettos surrounding the hotel strip, and since victims of prejudice seem susceptible to the disease themselves, Atlantic City just packed up and moved to Florida. The Jersey shore was desolate; Mr Peanut stopped dancing, as did the coloured waters; the burlesque house closed, and salt-water taffy became extinct.

The owner of the Majestic, Mr Feldstein, asked me to become his partner in a new hotel in the booming Sunshine State. He couldn't afford to lose Rose Rose. So the Double Rose Hotel opened on Collins Avenue. We promised double the comfort, double the sea air, and our old Majestic customers came flocking. The dining room was once again open for dinner, only further south. And every so often, Abbie and I would turn on the television on our tropical veranda in Miami Beach and watch, on the news, an abandoned palace-hotel in Atlantic City being demolished. The boardwalk was littered with rubble, like the streets of Dresden, where I once saw a child with no arms.

Takes a long drink of water and then puts it down, refreshed.

Each summer a group of young Israelis came to our hotel and gave us a presentation. It's unfair to say that they were aglow with youth, because it was so much more than that; there was a passion and belief in the future that I had not encountered before. Future wasn't even a concept in Yultishka or Warsaw or even in Atlantic City or Miami; on some subconscious level we knew we were skipping over quicksand. But the Israelis seemed to lack subconscious; they were entirely up front and present with no dark or hidden corners. They showed us slides of their kibbutz, they sang and danced the hora and collected money from our guests and each time they urged us to follow them back to join them in their great adventure and each time I wanted to, I wanted to be on the edge again, I wanted to dangle over a crevice with a very slender rope, but now I was a Rose Rose with responsibilities, so instead I gave money to plant trees in the names of my family. It seemed fitting to make mama into a tree, although they couldn't promise me lilac. Abbie made friends with the Israelis, especially a young couple named Noam and Rutie, and when he was sixteen I let him spend the summer on their kibbutz. He left with acne and returned with a clear complexion and I knew he had discovered not only olive groves and irrigation ditches but sex as well.

Two summers later Egypt invaded Israel. Abbie begged me to give him the air fare to Tel Aviv. How could I refuse? His father was only a few years older when he ran off to *The Exodus*. Abbie went to Noam's kibbutz and worked in the fields while the men were away. It famously took Israel six days to win the war. It was unreal. Miami Beach was jubilant. We had an all-night party at the Double Rose. We were all warriors. There would be no screams behind a wall again. *The Exodus* would not be towed away again. I cried that night as I hadn't in years, but I wasn't sure why. Abbie phoned me. He wanted to stay. I wasn't surprised.

I told Sonny our child was living on a kibbutz; that he had, in essence, achieved our dream for us. Sonny's hands shook, his eyes were vacant, the nurse fussed. Did he understand how the world had changed? A few months later his heart gave up. I sat shivah and mourned not his death but his life.

Abbie returned for the funeral and promptly fell in love with a young nurse from Sonny's hospital. She was blonde and sweet and, as her name was Kim, definitely not Jewish. One of Christianity's more interesting contributions to twentieth-century culture was names like Kim. Abbie stayed on to court her, and soon Kim was as much in love with Abbie's dream as Abbie himself. She took instruction and converted to Judaism and changed her name to Chava and they were

married under a chuppah at the Double Rose and soon, as
if it hadn't happened at all, they were gone.

I was alone. My husband was dead, my son was gone.
Sonny had been a vegetable for years, but at least he was
my vegetable. Abbie stopped listening to me some time ago,
but it was my voice he was ignoring. Now there was silence.
Not even the sewers were silent – rats make noise. People
talked all the time in the hotel, but their sounds blended and
I heard nothing.

Except for Bessie Goodman. I heard Bessie Goodman
because she never spoke. She drove the staff crazy. It was the
styrofoam boxes, I imagine. Bessie placed her meals – three
meals a day – into styrofoam boxes. Well, most of her meals.
She did nibble a little in the dining room, but only a little,
and then – woosh – food into box. Coffee as well; liquid
didn't faze her. She kept the boxes in a small freezer in her
room. Soon there were too many boxes for the freezer. Her
room became a shrine to decaying chopped liver and gefilte
fish. I didn't have to ask why; I saw The Old Country
stamped on her brow. She was storing supplies. I sat with her
in her room, in absolute silence. We both knew. But Mr
Feldstein anticipated a health crisis and he sent for her son.

Morton Goodman arrived at the hotel with a group of
friends. They wore outrageous colours and beads and they
all had musical instruments. They were, in fact, a band. The
name of the band was MORT and they sang about death, a
subject they knew nothing about. To them, death was what
you did after life. MORT went to Bessie's room and played
for her. They sang their entire repertoire. Finally she
couldn't take it any longer. She threw out the styrofoam
boxes. MORT emerged victorious.

Morton thanked me for being kind to his mother. He took
my hand. His shirt was open and I noticed his chest was
smooth. Uh-oh. He was twenty-eight. I was forty-eight, big
deal, barely old enough to be his mother . . .

Laughs.

Oh well. We became lovers. I started wearing beads. I bought a guitar. The hotel guests became restive. Bessie Goodman started losing weight. I threw away my bra. Mr Feldstein suggested I took a few months' leave. It would be good for my head. What a hip phrase, I thought.

I went to Connecticut and moved into a commune with Morton and his friends. There were twelve of us in an empty loft. We smoked a lot of dope and talked about peace and love and noble things and I did not mention the last time I lived twelve to a room lest I blacken their innocence. They called me Cool Mama and Morton wrote a song for me. 'Rose Is A Rose'. He claimed not to have heard of Gertrude Stein. There were long conversations into the night, intense and blurry; as if Asher and his fellow Yeshiva students were high on marijuana. I didn't have to hide my obsessive reading habits from them, as I did at the hotel. I felt free to enjoy language within a new culture that was, in its own way, destroying it.

Almost everyone in the commune was Jewish but that seemed to play no part in their identity. We discussed Buddha and karma instead of Rabbi Emanuel of Minsk, we went to ashrams instead of shul, and recited mantras instead of kaddish. Morton and I went away to meditate, to an ashram run by Ran To Poy, the former Seymour Goldstein. I tried to empty my mind. I couldn't. Nothing in my background prepared me not to think, not to question, not to somehow confuse the issue. My past kept floating through my head. I didn't welcome the memories but I couldn't pretend they didn't exist and I couldn't pretend I wasn't Jewish. It was just some kind of DNA in my bones. I left Ram To Poy and I left Morton. I told him I was too old. He thought I meant age. I couldn't explain. Mr Feldstein welcomed me back with a relieved grin. He was a kind man. Two years later, I married him.

Abbie and Chava had a family. Rafi first, then Irit, then Doron, beautiful children, born with the olive features of their land, as if the earth itself had conceived them. I went to visit. My first time since I kissed the ground. It wasn't like my memory. I fell in love with the land, with the desert and the hills and the amazing sense of green, green planted by pioneers, green transforming an arid earth. I loved too the feeling that everyone, absolutely everyone, in the country looked like my relative; even, in some odd way, the unamused faces in the small Arab villages we drove hurriedly through; there was something in their eyes that I recognized, a look I remembered from the sardines on *The Exodus*. When I arrived at the airport, Abbie said Welcome home, Mama, and of course he was right. It was home, and I cried when he said it, and I cried when I left, two weeks later, for Miami Beach and my husband and my hotel.

Actually, the hotel wasn't doing so well. Many of our customers had died; others were now too old to have anything to take a vacation from. The neighbourhood had changed as well; it had suddenly become Cuban, with loud salsa music, which was nice, and cocaine dealers, which wasn't. I suggested we convert the hotel into a retirement home; our guests could just stay on for ever, and end their days quietly by the sea, albeit to a Latin beat, with the occasional sound of bullets to spice up the night air. We redecorated and hired nurses and Double Rose was in business again. Mr Feldstein and I had our own apartment nearby; he was an amiable companion, and he knew to leave me alone when I had my moods, when, once or twice a year, I would retreat into my room and wonder why I went to the factory that day so long ago. But eventually, I would play 'Rose Is A Rose' on my Walkman – MORT had become successful and the song a hit – and I would think how strange it all was and then open my door and return to a semblance of life.

Every summer I returned to Israel. It was changing. The milk was slightly sour, the honey a bit tart. There was a war on, a few miles away, in Lebanon, and Jews were being killed again, but this time Jews were killing as well, and we weren't really sure if it was in self-defence, and we saw photographs of women and children picking their way through the rubble and the rubble wasn't ours, it was next door, and we were confused, and our little boys had grown and started a beard and had wet dreams and carried a gun and marched down the road into another land. Abbie and his friends on the kibbutz hated it. Noam and Rutie were in despair; they were sabras, after all, they had virtually created this land, but not for this, they said, not for this. Chava, however, was fervently in favour of the war. Chava/Kim had the passion of the converted. She knew what the Bible said about enemies. She became increasingly religious. She began to keep a kosher house. She cut off her hair and wore a wig. Abbie was appalled then confused then hostile. The kibbutzniks and the religious despised each other. I did not really understand. Abbie and Chava did not look for common ground; they pushed each other away. Their house was choking with tension.

One day a theatre in Haifa brought a play to the kibbutz. It was a play designed for a young audience and indeed it was about teenagers in the Warsaw ghetto. Rafi, Irit and Doron wanted me to go with them. I had no desire to revisit the ghetto, even in make-believe. Enough already. But I did want my grandchildren to understand our past. OK, I thought, knowledge is more important than pain, so I went.

The auditorium was filled with eager young faces. Onstage was an imitation ghetto, a little too pretty, a little too tidy. There was no stench. It was utterly foreign to the audience, it could have been a fairy tale. Where was the smell, I wondered. At one point in the action a teenage boy leaves his home to go underground and fight the Nazis – was it as simple as that, I thought, was it? – and his grandmother, an old, fat lady wearing a babushka and talking with a heavy accent, calls after him, using his Yiddish name. Yitsalah, she calls. Yitsalah. A strange noise began to circulate through the audience. Yitsalah, she called. The noise grew louder. Yitsalah, Yitsalah. Suddenly the sound was crashing around me like a tidal wave waiting to sweep me out to sea. Laughter. The kids were laughing. The kids from the kibbutz were laughing at the name, laughing at Yitsalah, laughing at Yiddish, laughing at the grandmother, laughing at the moon, for what the grandmother represented might as well have been the moon. Yitsalah, Yitsalah. The audience repeated the name now, jabbing each other with their elbows. My grandchildren were laughing too. Rafi looked at me, wondering why I wasn't joining in. I was wearing a bright summer dress and you could see my breasts and they were still firm and my hair was dyed a soft brown with an occasional blonde streak, so what could I possibly have to do with the woman in the babushka? With Yitsalah? I began to cry and Rafi was no longer concerned for he thought he saw tears of laughter.

They thought it was funny, I said to Abbie later. So what? he replied. It's their culture, I said. No longer, he replied, and certainly not if they're Sephardic or African. Anyhow, we don't speak Yiddish here, Mama, didn't you notice? We speak Hebrew. Yiddish was unnatural, a mutant, a mongrel; medieval German and a bit of Russian and Turkish and French mixed together in a blender and then you added a little seasoning and spice, whereas Hebrew is the language of Abraham, Isaac and Jacob, Hebrew is our very source, and, finally, after all these years, we have reclaimed it. I was stunned. I actually thought his description of Yiddish beautiful and explained why it was so special. On the other hand, I understood his meaning, and from his perspective, he wasn't wrong. He was marching into the future, wasn't he? Oh that word – future. Every conversation about Israel had that word in it. Still, how could I argue? Well, I tried. It does represent something, I said, an entire civilization, a way of life, a way of thinking that's inspired this novel and that symphony and a theory of relativity and a science about the subconscious and maybe even ideas about collective living that have in turn inspired your kibbutz, and if it is lost completely, if it is utterly wiped away, then isn't that Hitler's Final Victory? That's just meshugge, he replied. I looked at my son. Meshugge is a Yiddish word, I said. He laughed and walked away.

Time passed. I stopped dying my hair. The Double Rose
began to lose money; among the many things old age isn't
is profitable. Mr Feldstein had a heart attack. I nursed him
for two years and then he passed on. I finally sat shivah for
someone who had not died before their time – it made me
feel so grown up. Meanwhile, Miami Beach had
transformed yet again, and was suddenly – overnight – the
chic and swinging centre of America. Art shmeco had
risen from the dead, and Collins Avenue was prime real
estate. I sold Double Rose for a fortune. The new owners
liked the name, so now Double Rose is the hottest club in
town, filled with gymnasium bodies and a drug called
Ecstasy.

I kept my apartment, it's good for them to see an old
person, I figured, and besides Rafi likes to visit me here.
Rafi and his sister Irit left Israel some years ago. Their
parents had divorced by then. Chava remarried – a settler
on the West Bank, a man with a Bible, a beard and a B-59.
Irit moved to Rome, married a Catholic writer, and had two
children, neither of whom are raised as Jews. Rafi moved to
Los Angeles. He's a film editor. He has – do I have to say it
– long hair and an earring, and, in addition, a boyfriend.

A few years ago I went to visit Rafi in Los Angeles; he
showed me how he worked. Once I understood about fast
forward and jump-cutting I realized that there was nothing
unusual about my hallucinations and that movies were just
catching up with our minds. Rafi took me to a hill that
overlooked his city, and I told him that this abnormal
metropolis exists as it is because a dozen immigrants – Jews
from The Old Country – made their way here seventy-five
years ago and founded an industry, what people called a
dream factory, and that in turn created our image of
American culture, it printed visions on our minds, cossacks
riding through the shtetl became Indians attacking a wagon
train, and those images seeped into all the existing cultures
around the world, corrupting them, enriching them,
changing them for ever, and it was all a fantasy of these little
schlemiels, the Mayers and Zukors and Warners and

Goldwyns, Goldwyn being originally Goldfish, who had a cousin who knew my father's sister in a little village in the Ukraine which now lies beneath the Chernobyl dust. Rafi's eyes glazed over; it didn't interest him. I hugged him anyway.

That's when we went to Arizona. I wanted to see the real West. It wasn't so real. There were no cowboys or Indians, no stagecoaches riding around the bend, just airless towns and unending desert and an occasional technicolour canyon. One day we drove for hours in emptiness. Wherever you looked was nothing and the scale of nothing was awesome. Finally we reached a little souvenir shop that stood alone in the nothing. Rafi's car was overheating. He went inside for some water. I walked around the front of the store. The windows were covered with tired, touristy watercolours of the desert. I walked inside. A wooden Indian stood in an aisle. He held a cigar. There was a price tag on him and above the price the words original, not a copy. An old man stood behind the counter, minus a price tag. He was shouting at his son in the stockroom. The son was middle-aged and disturbed; desolate, I would say. The old man's voice was too rough. I could hear a slight accent. I looked at some more watercolours. They were terrible. Rafi and the old man were arguing. The old man refused to give Rafi water. I joined Rafi at the counter. Maybe an old lady would get some water. I noticed the old man's hands. They were filthy and chapped by the sun. Then I saw his arm. There was a faded number tattooed on it. I felt dizzy. I would never have expected that in Arizona, in the middle of nothing. The old man was shouting at his son again, as well as Rafi. I wanted him to shut up. My gaze swept up his arm to his stomach, which was gross, and his neck, which was sagging, and then to his face, which was like leather, and his eye, his false eye, his false eye that looked through me, and his other eye, the real one, the blue one, that seemed more like a heart than an eye, a heart that had shattered a long time ago. We looked at each other and did not speak. And then I turned and ran out of the store, past the wooden

Indian and the dreadful watercolours, back into the nothing.
I stared at nothing for a long time, then returned to the car.
Rafi sat down beside me, a pail of water on his lap. He
asked me what was wrong. I could not answer. I looked out
of the car window and saw, coming toward us, across the
prairie, a rolling tumbleweed. It blew past our car and out
again into the desert and disappeared.

Pause.

Even though the doctor doesn't believe me about the
breathing he insists it helps to sip water all the time. I forget
to sip. I forget.

She pours another glass of water, and drinks a bit.

I don't remember what I was talking about.

Pause.

Oh yes. Shivah.

Pause.

Abbie is angry at me. For sitting shivah. He was on the
phone this morning screaming at me from Tel Aviv. He
lives in Tel Aviv now that his kibbutz has gone kaput. It's
not your business, he said. You are not one of us. And he's
right. On the other hand . . .

Sips some water.

Chava lives on the West Bank on a little settlement that
adjoins an ancient Palestinian village. Fig trees and rock. It
is, of course, in the Bible, an ancient Hebrew village as well.
She took Doron, her youngest, with her when she left
Abbie. I went to visit several years ago. I wanted to see my
grandson, who was still the sweetest boy, but it was odd
being on land that didn't want me, where I felt that,
ethically, I didn't belong. I remembered how we celebrated
the six-day victory in Miami Beach and how, years later,
Noam and Rutie, drinking too much one night in the
kibbutz, told me that the spoils of war were a curse. I didn't
want to be there.

Chava did not make it easier. She kept saying forefathers, forefathers this, forefathers that, and then in front of my grandchild, she would praise the memory of this man, this Baruch someone, who massacred a group of worshippers at the Hebron mosque. I told Chava that was sinful. She reminded me of the countless Jews who were themselves massacred on this land. I know, I know, I said, and I mourn them with a depth that even you cannot understand, and I will mourn again when it happens again, but that still does not excuse this Baruch person. We're supposed to be better than that. We're supposed to carry a moral light unto the world. We, we, she screamed, how can you say we, you don't deserve to call yourself a Jew. I thought, well – just about the time my entire family was wiped out because they were Jewish you, my dear, were being baptized in Kansas.

I didn't stay too long and I didn't see Doron again until last night, when I put on the television news and I saw his sweet, handsome face, sweaty and strained and defiant. There had been a riot. The settlers and the villagers. Someone attacked someone. Someone threw a stone. Someone was knifed. A settler fired at the villagers. A little girl had been swept up in the crowd. Well, maybe. Maybe she had been throwing a stone. She was nine. A bullet struck her in the forehead. It caught her in the middle of a thought. Her name was Nora. Nora el-Kareem. They interviewed the man who fired the shot. He wasn't a man. He was a sweet-faced boy. Doron. My blood. Son of Yultishka. Son of the lilac tree. Child of Warsaw. Doron. He killed a little girl. He killed Nora el-Kareem. His grandfather sailed a ship to a promised land. Doron. My blood.

So today I sit shivah for Nora el-Kareem. The last of my shivahs. It is, of course, a totally empty gesture; I know that, but I had to do something. At first I thought I would write to her parents and tell them I was mourning their child, but they would hate me for patronizing them, just as I would have hated the grandmother of the soldier who shot Esther had she dared to make a gesture toward me. Esther, who I never really mourned – I was too busy staying alive; Esther, who I never sat shivah for on a proper wooden bench. Now I'm sitting shivah for a little girl and it is meaningless. A little girl who died with Palestine on her lips. I talk to Nora in Yiddish. It's all right, bubeleh, I say, it's all right.

Abbie is furious. Why are you doing this, he asks. Because it's wrong. Jews don't kill little girls. Everyone kills little girls, he shouts. It is horrible, but every nation does it. But you are still occupying territory, I say. Yes we are, he replies, and although it is not nearly as simplistic as you make it out to be, I strongly object to it; in fact, it tears me in half and I know that if we don't solve this soon we are all, all of us, headed for disaster, but it is our problem, my problem, not yours. But Israel belongs to every Jew, I say. Only in theory, he replies. What did you do, you bought a few trees, you sent some money, you paid a few visits, but did you taste it every day? It's the difference between casual sex and a relationship, he says, It could have been yours, you kissed the ground before any of us, but you chose to live as an outsider, a very comfortable one, but an outsider nonetheless, just as your ancestors did for centuries. So I'll condemn my own son if I choose to, and I do choose to, but here in my own country. I won't let the rest of the world tell my son if he's wrong or right. And I won't let you tell me that Jews have to be better than everyone else. But I'm not the rest of the world, I say, I'm part of you. No, you're part of chopped liver and dybbuks, he replies, that's something different, that's the past, this is the future. I know you hate that word, but it is our only future. We have nothing else. Do you understand? Everything else is gone. And then suddenly he starts to cry. My Abbie starts to cry. You have to let us go, Mama. Your shadows will choke us to death. We can't carry you with us. Your world is dead. And then he's silent. I can tell he's embarrassed. And then he says, You only think you're sitting shivah for this girl. That's not what you're sitting shivah for. What then, I ask. You tell me, he says.

Finishes sipping the water.

There's no more water.

Turns the glass upside down.

What was I saying?

Pause.

I should get another bottle. I haven't the energy. I hear laughter outside. Night-time in Miami Beach. Someone is always having a good time. Probably chemically-induced. I don't belong here, Abbie is right. But there was always a joy in not belonging. Did I belong in Yultishka? Or Warsaw? Or anywhere? Restless minds . . . what did I say? . . . a restless people produce restless minds.

Pause.

Maybe God is just a question like everything else.

Pause.

I'm thirsty, The truth is wooden benches are very uncomfortable. But I have to mourn a little girl, don't I? It's all right, bubeleh, it's all right. Sleep my child, sleep. Sweet Nora. My Esther. Shall I sing you a song? Of course, that's the other thing about sitting shivah, you can sing songs. How about a song from a movie? A movie I saw in Warsaw on Krochmalna Street. With Yussel. We had just been to a café. I think there was some kind of fight. Over poetry. How stupid. No, maybe someone owed someone else money. Or had slept with someone's friend. I don't remember. Anyhow, in the movie, Molly Picon was making a fool of herself. It took place in a shtetl, but it was a shtetl made of cardboard. It was a set. Or maybe it was Yultishka. Yussel put his hand under my blouse while she sang.

Sings.

    'Yiddle mit a fiddle . . .
    Yiddle, Yiddle, Yiddle . . .'

Stops.

And his hand pinched my breast . . .

Pause.

What was I saying?

Pause.

Sings.

  'Yiddle, Yiddle, Yiddle . . .'

Pause.

I think that song is a silly thing to remember. On the other hand . . .

She gasps.

She suddenly cannot catch her breath.

She closes her eyes . . .